# SNAKES

# *Rat Snakes*

by Linda George

**Consultants:**
The staff of Black Hills Reptile Gardens
Rapid City, South Dakota

CAPSTONE
HIGH-INTEREST
BOOKS

an imprint of Capstone Press
Mankato, Minnesota

Capstone High-Interest Books are published by Capstone Press
151 Good Counsel Drive, P.O. Box 669, Mankato, Minnesota 56002
http://www.capstone-press.com

*Library of Congress Cataloging-in-Publication Data*
George, Linda.
    Rat Snakes/by Linda George.
    p. cm.—(Snakes)
    Includes bibliographical references (p. 45) and index.
    ISBN 0-7368-0909-0
    1. Rat snakes—Juvenile literature. [1. Rat snakes. 2. Snakes.] I. Title.
II. Animals and the environment. Snakes.
QL666.O636 G463 2002
597.96'2—dc21                                                2001000047

Summary: Describes the physical attributes, habitat, and hunting and mating methods of rat snakes.

**Editorial Credits**
Blake Hoena, editor; Lois Wallentine, product planning editor; Timothy Halldin, cover designer and illustrator; Katy Kudela, photo researcher

**Photo Credits**
A. B. Sheldon/Root Resources, 17, 30, 36
Allen Blake Sheldon, 6, 9, 13, 32
Bill Beatty/Visuals Unlimited, 26
David G. Campbell/Visuals Unlimited, 44
Jim Merli/Visuals Unlimited, cover, 20, 24
Joe McDonald/TOM STACK & ASSOCIATES, 14, 35
Laurie Grassel, 18–19, 40
Rick and Nora Bowers/Visuals Unlimited, 23
Rob and Ann Simpson, 29, 39
Unicorn Stock Photos/Rob and Ann Simpson, 10

2  3  4  5  6  07  06  05  04  03  02

# Table of Contents

Yellow areas represent the rat snake's range.

# Fast Facts about Rat Snakes

**Scientific Name:** Rat snakes are members of the Colubridae family. Most rat snakes belong to the *Elaphe* genus within this family.

**Size:** Most rat snakes average between 3 and 5 feet (.9 and 1.5 meters) long.

**Range:** Rat snakes live in North and South America, Europe, and Asia.

| | |
|---|---|
| **Description:** | Rat snakes have a flat underbelly. This shape helps them climb well. They have a broad and square head. Their skin can be a variety of colors and patterns. |
| **Habitat:** | Rat snakes live mainly in wooded areas and areas around farm buildings where rats and mice are plentiful. |
| **Food:** | Rat snakes eat mice and rats. They also may eat eggs, birds, frogs, and other small animals. |
| **Habits:** | Rat snakes may give off a foul-smelling substance if picked up or bothered. Rat snakes shake their tail when threatened. This action makes a sound similar to the sound rattlesnakes make. |
| **Reproduction:** | Male rat snakes engage in a combat dance before mating. The winner mates with the female. Female rat snakes lay up to 30 eggs at a time. Rat snake hatchlings are 7 to 14 inches (18 to 36 centimeters) long. |

# CHAPTER 1

# *Rat Snakes*

Rat snakes get their name from one of the animals that they eat as food. Rat snakes are well known for eating rodents such as rats. But rat snakes also eat eggs, birds, lizards, and other small animals.

## Snake Families

All snakes are reptiles. Alligators, crocodiles, lizards, and turtles also are reptiles.

More than 2,300 snake species exist in the world. A species is a specific type of animal or plant.

Scientists divide snake species with similar features into families. Rat snakes are members

**Rat snakes are members of the Colubridae family.**

of the Colubridae family. This group also includes king snakes and whip snakes.

The Colubridae family is the largest snake family. It contains more than 1,000 different snake species. Snakes in the Colubridae family mostly are non-venomous. Venomous snakes inject venom into their prey when they bite. Snakes in the Colubridae family vary greatly in color, size, and shape.

## Rat Snake Genera

Scientists further divide snake families into genera. Most rat snakes are members of the *Elaphe* genus. This genus includes more than 50 rat snake species.

Scientists list some species of rat snakes in other genera. Scientists may reclassify snakes after they do more research on them. Scientists sometimes discover differences between snakes in a genus. They then may put these snakes in a different genus.

For example, the trans-Pecos rat snake was in the *Elaphe* genus. But now it is in the

The redtail rat snake is a member of the *Gonyosoma* genus.

*Bogertophis* genus. One reason for this change is that the trans-Pecos rat snake has scales beneath its eyes. Rat snakes in the *Elaphe* genus do not have these scales. The Baja rat snake also is in the *Bogertophis* genus. The green rat snake is in the *Senticolis* genus. The redtail rat snake is a member of the *Gonyosoma* genus.

# CHAPTER 2

# Rat Snake Species

More than 50 rat snake species exist. They vary greatly in size and color.

## Trans-Pecos Rat Snake

*Bogertophis subocularis* is the scientific name for the trans-Pecos rat snake. Scientists named this snake for the scales beneath its eyes. *Subocularis* means "beneath the eyes."

Trans-Pecos rat snakes have unusual eyes. Some people call these snakes "pop-eyed." Their eyes bulge out from their sockets. No other snake has this type of eyes.

Trans-Pecos rat snakes have black or dark brown H-shaped markings on their back.

**Trans-Pecos rat snakes have scales beneath their eyes.**

These markings form two dark stripes down the length of their body.

Most trans-Pecos rat snakes are between 2.5 and 4.5 feet (.8 and 1.4 meters) long. The longest recorded trans-Pecos snake was 5.5 feet (1.7 meters) long.

## Black Rat Snake

*Elaphe obsoleta obsoleta* is the scientific name for the black rat snake. These snakes are a subspecies of rat snake. They are closely related to other rat snakes such as Texas and yellow rat snakes. But black rat snakes have different color markings.

Young black rat snakes may have a white, yellow, orange, or red spotted pattern. But this coloring fades as they grow older. Adult black rat snakes are mostly black. Their underbelly may be gray, brown, or yellow.

Black rat snakes can grow to be 8 feet (2.4 meters) long. But most are less than 6 feet (1.8 meters) long.

**Adult black rat snakes are mostly black.**

## Texas Rat Snake

*Elaphe obsoleta lindheimeri* is the scientific name for the Texas rat snake. Texas rat snakes have yellow, gray, or brown coloring with dark stripes across their back. Their red skin often can be seen between their scales. They have a gray underbelly with dark spots. Most Texas rat snakes have a black head.

Most Texas rat snakes are between 3.5 and 6 feet (1.1 to 1.8 meters) long. But they can grow to be more than 7 feet (2.1 meters) long.

## Yellow Rat Snake

*Elaphe obsoleta quadrivittata* is the scientific name for the yellow rat snake. These snakes also are called chicken snakes, banded chicken snakes, yellow chicken snakes, or striped house snakes. Farmers often find them hunting rodents around chicken coops.

Yellow rat snakes are closely related to black and Texas rat snakes. But they are yellow in color. They have four black or dark brown

Yellow rat snakes have dark brown stripes.

stripes running down the length of their body. These stripes are on their back and sides. Yellow rat snakes can grow to be more than 6 feet (1.8 meters) long.

### Great Plains Rat Snake

*Elaphe emoryi* is the scientific name for the great plains rat snake. These snakes are light gray with brown, dark gray, or olive spots on their back. Two stripes intersect and form a diamond shape on their head.

Great plains rat snakes usually grow to be 2.5 to 3.5 feet (.8 to 1.1 meters) long. The largest recorded great plains rat snake was 5 feet (1.5 meters) long.

### Red Rat Snake

*Elaphe guttata* is the scientific name for the red rat snake. These snakes also are called corn snakes. People gave them this name because the checkered pattern on their underbelly looks like Indian corn. Another reason for this name is that red rat snakes often are found in corn cribs. They hunt rodents in these farm buildings.

**Great plains rat snakes are gray with dark spots.**

Red rat snakes are brightly colored. They usually are orange or yellow with large red spots on their back.

Most red rat snakes grow to be 2.5 to 4 feet (.8 to 1.2 meters) long. The longest recorded red rat snake was 6 feet (1.8 meters) long.

**Spots**

**Tail**

# Red Rat Snake

Head

# CHAPTER 3

# *Habitat*

Rat snakes live in many areas of the world. They live in North America, South America, Europe, and Asia. They also live on the islands of the Philippines, Japan, and Malaysia.

Most rat snakes live in wooded areas and areas around farm buildings. They often hunt rats and mice in these areas.

## North American Rat Snakes

Rat snakes are among the largest snakes in North America. They live in many areas of the continent.

**Trans-Pecos rat snakes live in rocky areas.**

Trans-Pecos rat snakes live in New Mexico, Texas, and Mexico. They live near the Pecos River. Trans-Pecos rat snakes stay near rocky areas. They can be found in the Chisos, the Guadalupe, and the Davis Mountains. Some people call these snakes Davis Mountain rat snakes.

Black rat snakes live in forests and rocky areas. They also can be found in abandoned buildings, wood piles, and trash dumps. They climb well and spend much of their time in large trees. Their range includes much of central and eastern United States.

Texas rat snakes live in wooded areas and pastures. They also live in swamps, marshes, and streams. They live in the southern United States from the Mississippi River to central Texas.

Yellow rat snakes live in river swamps. They climb well and spend time in trees. They often can be found near farm buildings. The yellow rat snake's range is from southern North Carolina to Florida.

**Texas rat snakes live in the southern United States.**

Great plains rat snakes live from Illinois west to Colorado and New Mexico. Their range also extends south to Texas and Mexico. They climb well and spend much of their time in trees.

Red rat snakes live from New Jersey south to Florida and west to Louisiana. Their habitats include pine barrens, wooded areas, and rocky

**Baja rat snakes live in Mexico.**

hillsides. They spend a great deal of time underground in burrows. They rest and hunt rodents in these underground tunnels.

### Other Rat Snakes

Several types of rat snakes live in Central America and Mexico. These snakes include the Baja rat snake and the Mexican rat snake.

The Mexican rat snake also is known as the nightsnake or tamaulipan rat snake. The Central American rat snake or Central American corn snake lives in countries along the coast of the Gulf of Mexico. These countries include Nicaragua, Honduras, Belize, and Guatemala.

Some rat snakes also live in Asia. The twin-spotted rat snake lives in southeastern China. Species of the Chinese king rat snake live in China, Vietnam, Taiwan, and Japan. This snake also is known as the stinking goddess. The Japanese rat snake and the red Japanese rat snake live in Japan.

Several types of rat snakes live in Europe. The Aesculapian rat snake lives in southern Europe and northern Iran and Turkey. Subspecies of the Aesculapian rat snake also live in Italy, Sicily, and Spain.

# CHAPTER 4

# *Hunting*

Rat snakes are known for eating rodents. But rat snakes will eat just about any living creature that they can catch and swallow. They will eat insects, frogs, lizards, birds, and eggs.

## Hunting Habits

Most rat snakes are nocturnal. They hunt and are most active at night. The animals that they hunt also are nocturnal.

Most rat snakes climb well. They are able to wedge their body between grooved or cracked surfaces such as the bark on a tree. They use the wide, flat scales on their underbelly to pull themselves upward. Their ability to climb

**Rat snakes can climb well.**

allows them to hunt birds in trees or find eggs in nests.

Rat snakes often ambush prey. They stay motionless for long periods of time and wait for prey to come near them. They then strike at their prey.

## Senses for Hunting

Snakes cannot see as well as people do. But rat snakes see better than most snakes. They can detect light, shapes, colors, and movement. This ability helps them find prey.

Snakes cannot hear sounds as people do. Instead, rat snakes are able to feel vibrations in the ground and in the air. These sensations help them know when prey is near.

The Jacobson's organ is located on the roof of a snake's mouth. Snakes use this organ to smell. A rat snake flicks out its tongue to collect scent particles in the air or on the ground. The tongue carries the scents to the Jacobson's organ. A rat snake can smell prey with its Jacobson's organ. A male rat snake also can smell females that are ready to mate.

Rat snakes uses their tongue to help them smell.

## Constriction

Rat snakes' teeth are curved toward the back of their mouth. This shape helps them hold on to prey.

Rat snakes are constrictors. They kill their prey by squeezing it to death. After catching prey, a rat snake quickly wraps its muscular

**A rat snake can eat animals that are larger than its mouth.**

body around the animal. It then squeezes its prey. A rat snake squeezes tighter each time its prey breathes out. This squeezing action prevents prey from breathing in. The prey then suffocates. It usually only takes a few minutes for a rat snake to kill its prey.

## Swallowing Prey

Rat snakes do not chew their food. They swallow prey whole. Rat snakes may swallow small prey while it is still alive.

A rat snake can swallow prey that is larger than its mouth. A rat snake's upper and lower jaws are connected by ligaments. These stretchy bands of tissue allow a rat snake to separate its jaws. Strong muscles in its throat then pull prey into its stomach.

Strong acids in a rat snake's stomach digest its prey. These chemicals break down food to be used by the body.

Many rat snakes eat eggs without breaking the shell. They swallow the eggs whole. The acids in their stomach then break down the egg's shell.

# CHAPTER 5

# *Mating*

Snakes are cold blooded. Their body temperature is similar to the temperature of their surroundings.

Rat snakes that live in cold climates must hibernate to survive. They burrow underground and remain inactive during the winter. This inactivity allows rat snakes to survive cold weather and lack of food.

Rat snakes wake from hibernation in the spring. They then start to look for a mate. Rat snakes have musk glands at the base of their tail. These organs leave a scent wherever the snakes go. Male snakes follow this scent trail to find females. More than one male rat snake

**Rat snakes hatch from eggs.**

may come across a female. The males then take part in a combat dance.

## Combat Dance

A combat dance determines which male rat snake mates with a female. The dance begins when one male rat snake tries to crawl past or over another male. The snakes then wrap their bodies around each other. They raise their heads and the front halves of their bodies high into the air. Each snake tries to climb on top of the other snake.

Eventually, one snake pushes the other snake down on the the ground. The winning snake holds down the losing snake for a moment. The loser then leaves. The winner mates with the female.

## Laying Eggs

Rat snakes are oviparous. Female rat snakes lay eggs that develop and hatch outside the female's body.

The female lays her eggs in early summer. It usually takes four to eight weeks for the eggs to

**Female rat snakes lay eggs.**

hatch. Hatchlings are between 7 and 14 inches (18 and 36 centimeters) long.

Adult rat snakes do not take care of their young. Young rat snakes must find their own food and shelter. They often eat insects, worms, and baby mice. Rat snakes reach adulthood after about three years.

# CHAPTER 6

# Rat Snakes and People

Rat snakes can be beneficial to people. They eat rats and mice. These rodents may spread diseases. Rats and mice also eat farmers' crops. Rat snakes help keep rodent populations down.

But rat snakes are not always helpful. They sometimes eat young chickens or chicken eggs. Farmers may try to kill rat snakes that eat their farm animals.

To kill rat snakes, some farmers place porcelain doorknobs in chicken nests. These glass doorknobs look similar to real eggs. A snake eats the doorknob along with the real

Rat snakes eat rodents.

eggs. The snake cannot digest the doorknob. It blocks the snake's food passage. The snake then dies.

## Pilot Snakes

People tell many myths about snakes. These stories are untrue.

People used to believe black rat snakes warned people about venomous snakes. They believed black rat snakes then guided people safely away from these snakes. Because of this myth, people called black rat snakes "pilot snakes."

In truth, black rat snakes sometimes hibernate with venomous snakes. Snake experts believe that this fact may have led to the "pilot snake" myth.

## Defenses

A rat snake may shake its tail against the ground or among dead leaves when threatened. The rough skin on a rat snake's tail can create a clicking or buzzing sound. This sound is similar to the sound a rattlesnake makes when it shakes its tail. Rattlesnakes are venomous snakes.

**Rat snakes sometimes shake their tail against the ground to create a rattling sound.**

A rattlesnake shakes its tail when threatened. This sound warns other animals that the rattlesnake is near and that it may bite. Animals may recognize rattlesnakes as dangerous. Some predators may mistake a rat snake for a rattlesnake because of the sound its tail makes. Animals then may avoid the rat snake.

When cornered, a rat snake raises the front part of its body. It draws its head back in an

S-curve and opens its mouth to strike. A rat snake may hiss as it lunges forward to strike.

A rat snake may give off a foul-smelling substance when threatened. The scent of this substance makes the rat snake seem distasteful to predators.

## Rat Snakes as Pets

Most rat snakes are not aggressive. They can be picked up and handled easily.

Many people believe that rat snakes make good pets. Even wild rat snakes become tame after being handled by people. But tame snakes may still bite if they are threatened.

Rat snakes are popular and beneficial snakes. Many people keep them as pets because of their non-aggressive nature and brightly colored patterns. Rat snakes also are beneficial because they eat rodents that may spread diseases and eat food crops.

**Many people believe rat snakes make good pets.**

# Words to Know

**acids** (ASS-ids)—substances in an animal's stomach that break down food

**ambush** (AM-bush)—to hide and then attack; rat snakes ambush their prey.

**constrict** (kuhn-STRIKT)—to squeeze

**digest** (dye-JEST)—to break down food so it can be used by the body

**family** (FAM-uh-lee)—a group of animals with similar features

**genus** (JEE-nuhss)—a group of related animal or plant species

**habitat** (HAB-uh-tat)—the place and natural conditions in which plants and animals live

**hatchling** (HACH-ling)—a recently hatched animal; rat snakes hatch from eggs.

**hibernate** (HYE-bur-nate)—to be inactive during the winter; rat snakes often hibernate by burrowing into the ground.

**ligament** (LIG-uh-muhnt)—a strong, stretchy band of tissue that connects bones

**nocturnal** (nok-TUR-nuhl)—active at night

**oviparous** (oh-VIP-uh-rus)—laying eggs that develop and hatch outside the female's body

**predator** (PRED-uh-tur)—an animal that hunts other animals for food

**prey** (PRAY)—an animal hunted by another animal for food

**species** (SPEE-sheez)—a specific type of animal or plant

**suffocate** (SUHF-uh-kate)—to kill by cutting off the supply of air or oxygen

**venom** (VEN-uhm)—poison produced by some snakes; venom is passed into a victim's body when venomous snakes bite.

# To Learn More

**Bartlett, R.D., and Patricia P. Bartlett.** *Corn Snakes and Other Rat Snakes.* A Complete Pet Owner's Manual. Hauppauge, N.Y.: Barron's, 1996.

**George, Linda.** *King Snakes.* Snakes. Mankato, Minn.: Capstone High-Interest Books, 2002.

**Ling, Mary, and Mary Atkinson.** *The Snake Book.* New York: DK Publishing, 1997.

**Mattison, Christopher.** *Snake.* New York: DK Publishing, 1999.

**Stone, Lynn M.** *Snakes That Squeeze and Snatch.* Eye to Eye with Snakes. Vero Beach, Fla.: Rourke, 2000.

# *Useful Addresses*

**Black Hills Reptile Gardens**
P.O. Box 620
Rapid City, SD  57709

**Milwaukee Public Museum**
Herpetology Department
800 West Wells Street
Milwaukee, WI  53233-1478

**National Zoological Park**
3001 Connecticut Avenue NW
Washington, DC  20008

**Toronto Zoo**
361A Old Firch Avenue
Scarborough, ON  M1B 5K7
Canada

# Internet Sites

**Black Hills Reptile Gardens**
http://www.reptile-gardens.com

**Enchanted Learning.com: Snake Printouts**
http://www.enchantedlearning.com/subjects/
  reptiles/snakes/printouts.shtml

**Ratsnakes of North America**
http://www.kingsnake.com/ratsnake

**Toronto Zoo**
http://www.torontozoo.com

# Index